Living
above the
AVERAGE

Living above the AVERAGE

Heroic Displays of Christlikeness

William MacDonald

GOSPEL FOLIO PRESS
304 Killaly St. West, Port Colborne, ON L3K 6A6
Available in the UK from JOHN RITCHIE LTD.
40 Beansburn, Kilmarnock, Scotland

All Scripture quotations are from the
New King James Version unless otherwise
indicated. New King James © 1979, 1980, 1982.
Thomas Nelson, Publisher

KJV   King James Version
RSV   Revised Standard Version
LB   Living Bible

Published by Gospel Folio Press
304 Killaly St. West
Port Colborne, ON L3K 6A6

ISBN 1-882701-76-3

Printed in the United States of America

Contents

If the way you live your life as a Christian can be explained in terms of *you*, what have you to offer to the man who lives next door? The way he lives his life can be explained in terms of *him*, and as far as he is concerned, you happen to be "religious"—but he is not! Christianity may be your hobby, but it is not his, and there is nothing about the way that you practice it which strikes him as at all remarkable. There is nothing about you which leaves him guessing, and nothing commendable of which he does not feel himself equally capable without the inconvenience of becoming a Christian.

—Major Ian Thomas

One

What Would Jesus Do?

After a night of prayer on a mountain, Jesus chose twelve disciples. He called them apostles because He was going to send them out to spread the gospel. The word *apostle* means "one who is sent."

When they descended, Jesus started to train them for their mission. First, He dealt with their lifestyle. They were to live sacrificially, to be serious about their calling, to be unpopular, and to suffer persecution for His sake.

Then He launched into a description of how they should behave.

I say to you who hear: Love your enemies, do good to those who hate you, bless those who curse you, and pray for those who spitefully use you. To him who strikes you on the one cheek, offer the other also. And from him who takes away your cloak, do not withhold your tunic either. Give to everyone who asks of you. And from him who takes away your goods do not ask them back. And just as you want men to do to you, you also do to them likewise.

But if you love those who love you, what credit is that to you? For even sinners love those who love them. And if you do good to those who do good to you, what credit is that to you? For even sinners do the same. And if you lend to those from whom you hope to receive back, what credit is that to you? For even sinners lend to sinners to receive as much back. But love your enemies, do good, and lend, hoping for nothing in return; and your reward will be great, and you will be sons of the Most High. For He is kind to the unthankful and evil. Therefore be merciful, just as your Father also is merciful (Luke 6:27-36).

What is your reaction to those commands of the Lord? Do you say, "Yes, that is what I believe. And that is what we Christians do." If you feel comfortable that we all live that way, I suggest that you read the passage again and be shocked by what it is saying.

What the Lord is teaching here is an otherworldly manner of life. It is behavior that is not natural. It is a walk that rises above flesh and blood, a life on a higher plane. Jesus is insisting that my life must be different from that of my neighbors. If I am not distinctive, I am saying to them, "Don't be afraid. I'm just like you are." If there is no difference, why should they listen to you when you seek to press the claims of Christ on them? It's the difference that matters. It's life above the average.

If, on the other hand, they see a big difference between my life and theirs, they are apt to seek for the reason and thus open the door for me to share the gospel with them. Major Ian Thomas, founder of the Torchbearers, says:

> It is only when your quality of life baffles the neighbors that you are likely to impress them. It has got to become patently obvious to others that the kind of life you are living is not only highly commendable, but that it is beyond all human explanation. That it is beyond the consequences of man's capacity to imitate, and however little they may understand this, clearly the consequences only of God's capacity to reproduce Himself in you.

> In a nutshell, this means that your fellow men must become convinced that the Lord Jesus Christ of whom you speak, is essentially Himself the ingredient of the life you live.[1]

Non-Christian people often perform great acts of heroism. They donate kidneys for nephritis victims. They take extraordinary care of aged parents. They give generously to charitable causes. We, however, are called to go beyond what is normal for the unsaved.

Having said all this, we must add that every time a Christian exhibits truly Christlike behavior, there is no guarantee that the unsaved will be won to the Savior. We are responsible to act as the Lord would have done, but unbelievers are still responsible to put their faith in Him. There will always be some who will turn away.

But that isn't all. If you wear Christ's coat well, there are those who will think you are mentally unhinged, that you've lost it. You can scarcely expect better treatment than He received. The disciple is not above his Master.

Years ago Russian novelist Fyodor Dostoevsky wrote a book[2] in which he tried to portray Prince Myshkin as a perfect specimen of humanity. The people couldn't understand the Prince. They thought he was out of his mind. The title of the book is *The Idiot*. The more we are conformed to the image of Christ, the more we run the risk of being known as idiots.

So the apostle Paul was right. We are a savor of *"life unto life"* for some, and a savor of *"death unto death"* for others. We either impress them by baffling them or confuse them by acting in a godly manner. In either event we reveal ourselves as sons of the Highest by imitating Him.

In the pages that follow, we will be thinking of several great moments in time when Christians took the sayings of Jesus literally by loving their enemies, forgiving their foes, returning good for ill, enduring without retaliating, giving without hope of return—in short, by asking themselves "What would Jesus do?" and then doing it.

Two

A Friend of God

Henry Suso was a German mystic who lived in the 1300s. He, Paul Tersteegen, and a few other devout believers were known as "The Friends of God." They were men who *"[dwelt] in the secret place of the Most High."* They were like the blessed man of Psalm 1 whose *"delight [was] in the law of the Lord, and in His law [they meditated] day and night."* Their citizenship was in heaven. The holiness of their lives was proverbial.

One day there was a knock on Suso's door. When he opened it, a woman whom he had never seen before stood there with a baby in her arms. Without warning she shoved the baby into his arms, saying, "Here you have the fruit of your sin," and walked off.

Suso was dazed. Her unfounded charge hit him like a bolt

of lightning. He stood there with a tiny infant in his arms. No doubt the child was the fruit of her sin, but it wasn't his. Today she might have put the baby in a plastic bag and deposited it in a dumpster. But to her it was more important to put the blame on someone else.

News of the incident quickly spread throughout the town, exposing Suso to the charge of being a religious fraud. But he was neither a hypocrite nor a fraud. All he could do was retreat and cry to the Lord.

"What shall I do, Lord? You know I'm innocent."

The answer came back to him clearly and plainly: "Do as I did; suffer for the sins of others, and say nothing." Suso got a fresh view of the Cross, and peace came to his soul.

He raised the baby as if it were his own, never once defending himself against the charge.

Years later the sinful woman returned to the town and told the people that Suso was innocent, that her accusation against him was false. The harm was done, but God turned it out for good. Suso had become even more conformed to the image of Christ. He had won the victory.

We read in the Old Testament that Joseph experienced the heartache and injustice of being falsely accused. The seductress charged him with attempted rape, even producing his coat as proof of his supposed sin. Yet he committed his case to the Lord, depending on Him for vindication.

The Lord Jesus was falsely accused. His enemies insisted He was born out of wedlock. They maintained that He performed His miracles by the power of Satan. They charged Him with subverting the Roman government. Yet He was able to say in the most difficult times *"Even so, Father, for so it seemed good in Your sight."*

We learn from His example that we don't need to justify ourselves or resort to legal relief. God allows sin to work itself out, exposing the accuser, and honoring the victim.

Three

An Apostle of Love[3]

Young Robert Chapman was brought up in a family of wealth, with a luxurious house, a staff of servants, and a vehicle bearing the family coat of arms on the side. The family was religious but not soundly Christian.

When he was twenty, a friend invited him to hear James Harrington Evans preach. It was a turning point in Chapman's life. He was converted to God within a few days.

He saw from the New Testament that believers should be baptized, so he asked Mr. Evans to baptize him. The cautious preacher said, "Don't you think you should wait a while and consider the matter?"

Chapman replied, "No, I think I should hurry to obey the Lord's commandment." That no-nonsense, obedient spirit went with him through life.

Although he became a successful lawyer, he felt that the Lord was calling him to full-time Christian work. He had no peace until he forsook all to follow Christ. In his case, forsaking "all" meant selling his possessions, giving away a fortune, and turning his back on the status and prestige of his legal practice. His ambition was to work among the poor. After all, *"Has God not chosen the poor of this world to be rich in faith and heirs of the kingdom which He promised to those who love Him?"* (James 2:5). Shouldn't the poor have the gospel preached to them (Matthew 11:5)? And didn't the common people hear Jesus gladly (Mark 12:37)?

People saw this "tall, smiling-faced young lawyer tenderly leading along a poor, decrepit, blind woman who had no one else to take her to the services. As they came down the aisle together, they were a living rebuke to those who, while sound in doctrine, were selfish and unloving in practice."

Eventually Chapman moved to a slum area in Barnstaple, England, to reach the down-and-outers. It was a scene of drunkenness, filth, alley rats, disease-ridden hovels, and poverty. Yet he ministered to the people constantly, and they were always welcome to come to his home.

He said, "There are many who preach Christ, but not so many who live Christ; my great aim will be to live Christ." Years later, John Nelson Darby said of him, "He lives what I preach."

When his overcoat became shabby, a Christian friend gave Chapman a new one, but the donor never saw him wear it. He had passed it on to a poor man who didn't have one. What puzzled Robert Chapman was that people thought this was extraordinary.

His relatives and friends were perplexed by his sacrificial lifestyle. One of them decided to visit him to see what was going on. When the taxi stopped in front of Chapman's house, the relative scolded the cabby:

"I told you to drive me to Mr. Chapman's house."
"This is the house, sir."

Once inside, the startled visitor said, "Robert, what are you doing here?"

"I am serving the Lord in the place to which He sent me."
"How do you live? Do you have a bank account?"

"I just trust the Lord and tell Him all I need. He never fails, and so my faith is increased, and the work continues."

The visitor saw that the pantry was practically empty so he offered to buy some food. Robert told him to go to a certain market. Actually the owner of the market had been bitterly hostile to Mr. Chapman. When this grocer was told to deliver the huge order of food to R. C. Chapman, he was overcome. He went straight to the Chapman home with the order, and, with tears and sincere repentance, he asked for forgiveness. In addition, he accepted Christ as his Lord and Savior.

Hospitality became an important part of the ministry. Chapman bought a house across the street from his own and asked the Lord to send guests of His choosing. There was no charge, and no one was asked when he planned to leave. The guests were told to put their shoes and boots outside their door each night. By morning, they were all polished. It was Mr. Chapman's way of washing the feet of his guests. This hospitality shown by a bachelor was designed to teach the guests about the life of faith and of service to the Lord's people. "There was great cheerfulness at the table—words of wisdom and grace were constantly heard; but no room was given for conversation to degenerate into frivolous talk. It was a rule of the house that no one should speak ill of an absent person, and any infringement of this rule called forth a firm though gracious reproof."

The virtue for which Robert Chapman was best known was love. One of his critics vowed that he would never have anything to do with him. He would never speak to him again. One day they found themselves walking down the sidewalk toward each other. Chapman knew all that the other man had said about him. But when they met, Robert put his arms around the man and said, "Dear brother, God loves you, Christ loves you, and I love you." The man repented and resumed fellowship in the assembly.

Incredible as it may seem, a friend in a foreign country mailed a letter addressed simply as: R. C. Chapman, University of Love, England. It was delivered.

Mr. Chapman did not like denominational divisions in the church, but he loved every true child of God, no matter what the church affiliation was. When a faction in his fellowship wanted to separate and claimed ownership of the property, he agreed to their demand. Then when the city government wanted a site that Chapman had purchased for an assembly, he yielded to the city. He would not take these matters to law, in spite of his own skill as a lawyer. In handling personal disputes, he avoided hasty action but resorted to prayer. Once when he chided J. N. Darby for acting precipitously, Darby defended his action by saying, "We waited six weeks." Chapman replied, "We would have waited six years."

Chapman led a disciplined life with time for prayer, reading the Word, meals, house to house visitation, feeding the hungry, helping the dispossessed, open air preaching, and Bible teaching. He fasted on Saturdays and worked on his lathe, making wooden plates as gifts for people.

One of his biographers, Frank Holmes, said of him: "For holy living, weight of character, and self-sacrifice, few can equal him; yet he was simple and humble as a child.... He was a spiritual giant. Not an inch of his stature was owed to the carnal methods of publicity experts."

Christ taught His disciples that their lives must be above the average if they were going to make an impact for Him. We see that fulfilled in the life of R. C. Chapman. One of his relatives was curious as to what caused Robert to follow such an out-of-this-world lifestyle. He realized that "inner forces of which he himself knew nothing drove Chapman." He determined to find out what he lacked. "He told Chapman quite frankly what his position was. The two had prayer and Bible study together. The result was that when the visitor went home, he was a changed man."

To our sophisticated age with its gimmicks and manipulative strategies, a man like Robert Chapman seems like a man from Mars, someone from another world. That is true. He was. He lived in the *"secret place of the Most High...under the shadow of the Almighty."* It was people like him of whom A. W. Tozer wrote:

> The truly spiritual man is indeed something of an oddity. He lives not for himself but to promote the interests of Another. He seeks to persuade people to give all to his Lord, and asks no portion or share for himself. He delights not to be honored but to see his Savior glorified in the eyes of others. His joy is to see his Lord promoted and himself neglected.

> He finds few who care to talk about that which is the supreme object of his interest, so he is often silent and preoccupied in the midst of noisy religious shoptalk. For this he earns the reputation of being dull and over-serious, so he

is avoided and the gulf between him and society widens. He searches for friends upon whose garments he can detect the smell of myrrh and aloes and cassia out of the ivory palaces, and finding few or none he, like Mary of old, keeps these things in his heart.[4]

May we make it our ambition to be truly spiritual believers in our generation.

Four

Great Peace in Sorrow [5]

Years ago H. A. Ironside told an unforgettable story about an Australian widow. This Christian lady was a woman of God. The depth of her spirituality was evident to everyone. Her life was marked by an unshakable faith in the Lord and by a profound submission to Him.

When her husband died, she was left with five sons to raise. She found strength in Psalm 146:9: *"He relieves the fatherless and widow."* It was a promise that she eagerly claimed. The boys had the great privilege of growing up in *"the training and admonition of the Lord."* In time, they all confessed Jesus Christ as Lord and Savior.

Then war broke out and the five young men answered the

call of their country. Perhaps it was by their own request that they were assigned to the same army regiment. Their mother committed them to the Lord day by day, knowing that their lives were in His care and keeping.

One day she looked out the window and saw a man walking up the path to the front door. She knew right away who it was. It was the minister who was the village chaplain, assigned to notify families when their loved ones were killed or missing in action. He, too, was a devout Christian, one who had a sad responsibility.

She went to the door and he stood there with a yellow cablegram in his hand. Time seemed to stand still. After they had exchanged greetings, she invited him in. When they sat down, she was finally able to ask:

"Which one?"

It was hard for him to answer. He feared that the news would be too much for her. But she was waiting, anxious to know which of her sons had fallen in combat.

Finally he got the words out: "All five of them."

Her face blanched. Her chin quivered. Her eyes filled

with tears. Then she said, with her typical trusting spirit: "They were all His. He has taken them to be with Himself."

Together they knelt in prayer.

"There was no hysteria, no murmuring, no bitterness, no complaint. She had entrusted her boys to a covenant-keeping God when they left their home at the call of their country, and she knew her Savior too well to question His love or His wisdom. Hers was the peace that passes understanding, and her testimony meant more in that village than all the sermons preached in years."

The story does not suggest that all believers can react in the same way that this Christian widow did. The Lord obviously gave her special grace for this overwhelming loss. To weep at the death of a loved one is neither shame nor failure. Even the Lord Jesus did that. But the incident shows that Christians are different in the hour of crushing sorrow, so different that the world looks on and is amazed. When believers appropriate the promises of God, they have hidden resources about which others know nothing.

Five

The Cost of Obedience

Life was a breeze for Bud Brunke. He had a loving wife, Janice, six children, and was a partner in an aircraft maintenance business at a small airport in Elgin, Illinois. The world was his oyster, or at least, so he thought.

Eventually, however, his peace was disturbed when thoughts of his spiritual condition began to trouble him. Up to that time, he had been a deacon and faithful member of the local Lutheran Church, but it did not satisfy him. The principal bone he had to pick with the church was infant baptism. He could no longer accept the idea that sprinkling water on an infant made that child a member of Christ and an inheritor of the kingdom of God. By a series of strange circumstances, he began to attend classes at an evening Bible school. In succeeding weeks, light dawned in his soul, and he became a committed

Christian while watching a telecast gospel crusade.

From the outset Bud had a keen desire to know the Word of God and to obey it. If he had thought that when he got saved, there would be no more problems, he was wrong. One problem in particular stood out. He was now in partnership with a man who was not a believer. This had never been a problem before. But now he read:

Do not be unequally yoked together with unbelievers. For what fellowship has righteousness with lawlessness? And what communion has light with darkness? And what accord has Christ with Belial? Or what part has a believer with an unbeliever? And what agreement has the temple of God with idols? For you are the temple of the living God. As God has said: "I will dwell in them and walk among them. I will be their God, and they shall be My people." Therefore "Come out from among them and be separate," says the Lord. Do not touch what is unclean, and I will receive you. I will be a Father to you, and you shall be My sons and daughters, says the Lord Almighty" (2 Corinthians 6:14-18).

The words stabbed Bud every time he read them. *"What part has a believer with an unbeliever?"* It was true. He and his partner were now on different wavelengths. They

32

had a different sense of values. Unethical practices had never been a problem before, but now they loomed large. It was as if an ox and a donkey were yoked together. They didn't pull together.

Bud knew what he should do. He should get out of the unequal yoke. But the aircraft maintenance business was his livelihood. He had to think about his family. They would have no visible means of support if he left. How would they live?

First, he decided to consult with an elder of a local assembly. He told the elder the whole story of how he was between a rock and a hard place.

The elder said, "There's no great problem here. Just buy out your partner so that you will be the sole owner of the business."

"I don't have enough money to do that."

"In that case, why don't you let him buy you out?"

That was worth investigating. He talked with the partner and, much to his surprise, the partner seemed agreeable to the idea. He promised to pay Bud $40,000 for his share in the business. It seemed like the ideal solution to the problem. The money started to dribble in. The monthly checks were for $200. Then the payments became sporadic. Later when Bud cashed the checks, they bounced back with the notation, "Insufficient funds."

It was no surprise when Bud learned that his former partner had filed for bankruptcy.

Bud's determination to obey the command, *"Do not be unequally yoked together with unbelievers"* had cost him between $38,000 and $40,000. What should he do? But God had not forgotten His promise, *"I will be a Father to you"* (2 Corinthians 6:18). Before long Bud went to work for a Christian, a position that lasted for 25 years. When he reached age 65 and retired, he received a payment that was three times what he had lost. It was just like the Lord. He is no man's debtor.

Six

The Brokenness that Wins[6]

David Akeman was a senior correspondent for one of the large newsmagazines, serving in Hong Kong. He had the reputation of being a committed Christian, one who was outspoken in his testimony for the Lord.

The bureau chief at that time was a constant irritation to Akeman because of his profane vocabulary. This man could hardly talk without taking the name of the Lord in vain. His conversation was invariably laced with oaths. Akeman tried to stifle his anger but the pressure built up inside.

Finally the safety valve blew. One day when this man's swearing was unusually offensive, Akeman barked, "Excuse me, I don't like the way you take the name of God in vain." He didn't say it quietly or graciously. Rather it was a harsh rebuke.

The bureau chief did not take it calmly. "Excuse me," he said, "I don't like the way you just said that to me."

At first David felt smug that he had finally brought the matter to a head. He had the satisfaction of telling this fellow off. Perhaps that would solve the problem. No longer would he have to listen to continual profanity. He had tackled a difficult problem and done it well.

But then he realized he had "blown it." What he had said to the boss was true enough, but the way he had said it was wrong. His testimony was tarnished. Communication between them had broken down.

As he lay in bed one night, he realized what he, as a Christian, had to do. He said, "I'm going to go there tomorrow and take complete blame for everything." It would be death to his pride. For him it would be a great humiliation. But he bit the bullet, and the next morning he stood before the bureau chief.

"I want you to know two things, and then I'll leave. Number one, our relationship has broken down. We're not communicating with each other, and the reason for that is me. I have not been the kind of person I should be. I take complete blame, and I beg your forgiveness. It's got nothing to do with you. It's me." The chief was stunned.

Now it was time to go the second mile.

"Number two," Akeman continued. "From now on, I give you first choice on every story. If you want to do a story, it's your choice. If you don't want to do it, I'll do it. Forgive me. The stories are all yours first, and I'll take the leftovers."

Such apology and unselfishness are virtually unknown in journalistic circles. The bureau chief was speechless. Akeman left the office, this time jubilant that he had restored the relationship.

A few days later, David heard about a Christian business-men's breakfast at which an executive was going to give his testimony of faith in Christ. Rather uncertainly he went to the bureau chief and said, "Look, I'm going to a breakfast where a businessman is going to tell about his belief in God. Would you like to go?" This time it was Akeman's turn to be surprised. "All right," his boss said. At the close of the meeting, he committed his life to Jesus Christ as his Lord and Savior.

Akeman commented, "He brought a lot of baggage with

him and is still battling it out. But if I had not taken that first move, I would never, ever have won this man over."

A full and unconditional apology like Akeman's is a rare commodity in this world's jungle. A renouncing of all rights is foreign in the competitive economy. Yet this is the kind of otherworldly behavior that wins tough men and women over to the Christian faith.

Seven

No Service Too Lowly [7]

God had called Doug Nichols to take the gospel to India; there was no doubt about it. The spiritual need of that country was staggering. Millions were under the grip of false religions. Doug was positive he had felt the divine tap on his shoulder.

If all that was true, what was he doing now, immobilized in the tuberculosis ward of a hospital, and a sub-standard hospital at that? It would have been easy to wonder why this illness had overtaken him. He could do so much more for the Lord if he were well.

Instead of succumbing to doubt and depression, however, he decided to evangelize the ward. He went from bed to bed, offering gospel tracts. The reception was unexpected. The other patients resented him. They looked on him as a rich American, occupying a bed in the hospital that might have been assigned to an Indian. They curtly refused his tracts.

The Lord had a different method for Doug to reach them with the Good News. One night a patient who was extremely weak and ill got out of bed with much difficulty. He wanted to go to the bathroom, but he was too weak to make it. He soiled himself and the floor, filling the ward with a horrible stench.

The nurses and maids turned on him, yelling curses because they had to clean up the mess. One actually slapped him. The whole incident made the patients squirm.

The next night, the pathetic sufferer tried to get out of bed again in order to go to the bathroom, but he was too weak. He fell back on the bed and wept.

In spite of his own weakness, Doug went over, picked up the man, and carried him to the bathroom. He waited until the man had relieved himself, then carried him back to his bed.

By that time, everyone was awakened and saw what had taken place. Their attitude toward the American intruder changed dramatically. One patient came to Doug's bed and offered a cup of hot tea, motioning that he wanted a tract. Doctors, nurses, and cleaning women asked for gospel booklets and the Gospel of John. Eventually some of them came to Christ because they had seen the Lord in the life and compassion of Doug Nichols.

This is what the Lord Jesus meant when He said that it is not enough to do kindnesses that the people of the world might do. We must go beyond that and show Christ in actions that are foreign to the world—supernatural demonstrations of love. If our behavior doesn't rise above the way the world acts, it will never make an impact on those who are perishing.

Eight

Scotland's Son Who Made Her Proud[8]

To understand Eric Liddell, you have to know that in the Scotland of his day, Christians respected and honored the Lord's Day. They called it the Christian Sabbath. They did no work, engaged in no sports, but faithfully attended the services of the church. Stores were closed and, except for emergencies, transportation facilities came to a halt. Believers set the day apart in a special way for the worship and service of the Lord. They reasoned that if you loved the Lord, you would love His day.

Eric made the greatest decision of his life when he was fifteen; he accepted Jesus Christ as his Lord and Savior. Even when he became passionate about running in races, the Lord was always his first priority.

He aspired to represent his country in the Olympics and his opportunity came in 1924 when he was chosen to run in the 100 meters event in Paris. He was elated. But that changed when a teammate told him that the event was to be held on a Sunday.

"It can't be," he groaned, "It can't be."

He sought out a quiet place and spent time in prayer. When he arose, he had a determined look. He would not dishonor the Lord and His day.

When this became known, it set off an uproar. "You have let your country down. You are a traitor." The manager of the British team cried, "You can't do this." He replied quietly, "I can't run on the Lord's Day."

His withdrawal made the headlines. The British athletic authorities were furious. The papers were ruthless in their condemnation. Some of his friends tried to defend him, but it was useless. The popular Eric was now a spoilsport.

Eric studied the bulletin board. He noticed that the 400 meters race was not being run on a Sunday. It wasn't his distance, but he could try. So he went to the manager and asked if he could run in it. Contrary to conventional policy, the manager agreed. Eric won in the first heat. He ran again and won. Soon he was in the semi-finals, then in the finals of what was considered the top event of the Olympics.

Before the race, the team masseur handed him a slip of paper. Eric read, "In the old book it says, *'Them that honour Me I will honour.'* Wishing you the best of success always." The Bible reference for the quote is 1 Samuel 2:30, KJV. The verse ran with him throughout the race.

An official who gave the British team a pep talk said, "To play the game is the only thing in life that matters." It was probably a rebuke aimed at Eric, but the arrow fell to the ground. To Eric there were other things that mattered more.

When the runners drew for their position in the lineup, Eric's was a bad one. In addition, the temperature that day was insufferable. It was unparalleled for the Olympics.

People said that Eric's running style was appalling. His arms were swinging, his fists punching the air, his knees pumping, and his head thrown back. Someone compared him to a windmill. But when he was about 50 meters from the goal, he made a supreme effort to increase his speed. He drew away from the other runners, won the gold medal, and set a new world's record.

One of his biographers wrote: "He captured the imagination of millions by tossing away his chance of a gold medal in the 100 meters—the race he was favored to win—because a principle of his Christian faith mattered more. When he unexpectedly won the 400 meters instead, the country was at his feet."[9] A prominent athlete said, "Without the slightest doubt, Eric was the greatest athlete Scotland has ever produced—by his influence, his example, and his capabilities."

Later he became a missionary in China. Before embarking, he said to his sister, "Jenny, God has made me for a purpose—for China; but He has also made me fast, and when I run, I feel His pleasure."

When the Japanese occupied China, Eric was sent to a concentration camp. Conditions were harsh. Food and clothing were scarce and the toilet facilities unspeakable. The camp brought out the worst in people. There was strife among many of the captives, especially American businessmen.

But there was agreement among them that Eric was different. "He lived his Christianity. He is portrayed as the Christ-figure here at the camp just as much as he was among the Chinese people in Siaochang. He befriends the prostitute and the despised businessman; he carries coal for the weak and teaches the young; he gets ready to sell his gold watch and tears up his sheets for hockey sticks. And yet he is still the same Eric, marching around in a multi-colored shirt made out of old curtains and looking extremely ordinary and nothing special at all."[10]

One of the internees, a Russian prostitute, needed some shelving. When Eric took care of it for her, she said that he was the first man who ever did anything for her without wanting to be repaid in kind.

One captive said of him, "I never heard Eric say an unkind word about anyone." Another testified, "Eric was the most Christlike man I knew."

When a Japanese guard noticed that Eric was not at roll call one day, someone explained that he had died a few hours earlier. The guard hesitated, then said, "Liddell was a Christian, wasn't he?" He had never talked to Eric but he must have seen Christ in him.

He died there, not as a result of brutality, but because of

a brain tumor. The camp clinic was not equipped to handle that kind of problem. Eric's last words, spoken to Annie Buchan, a Scottish nurse, were, "Annie, it's complete surrender."

When the news reached Glasgow, the *Evening News* announced: "Scotland has lost a son that did her proud every hour of his life."

At the funeral service, Arnold Bryson, one of the senior missionaries, said:

> Yesterday a man said to me, "Of all the men I have known, Eric Liddell was the one in whose character and life the spirit of Jesus Christ was pre-eminently manifested." And all of us who were privileged to know him with any intimacy echo this judgment. What was the secret of his consecrated life and far reaching influence? Absolute surrender to God's will as revealed in Jesus Christ. His was a God-controlled life and he followed his Master and Lord with a devotion that never flagged and with an intensity of purpose that made men see both the reality and power of true religion.[11]

There is a postscript to this story. In 1977, British movie director David Puttnam came across the story of Eric

Liddell's victory in the 1924 Olympics. Puttnam had just produced a film called *Midnight Express* that portrayed the worst in human nature. It was a cynical film that left a sour taste in his mouth. He was actually disappointed that it was such a triumph at the box office. Now he felt that Eric's story would serve as a catharsis. He said, "Here is a character who stands for something bigger than himself—putting duty to God before worldly success."

That is how the film *Chariots of Fire* came to be. It was an instant hit. People all over the world heard about a young man whose scruples meant more to him than a gold medal in the Olympics, a humble Scottish athlete who had firm convictions and would not compromise.

The film met wide acclaim. People wept as they watched how God honored a man who honored Him. New York film critic Rex Reed called it "one of the best movies ever made. It reaches deep for universal truths and expresses sentiments considered old-fashioned by today's cynical standards."

Eric ran the famous race in 1924. Fifty-seven years later the film came out that honored him in a way that he could never have imagined.

Nine

The General Who Humbled Himself [12]

The Civil War was over and preparations for a great victory parade in Washington were under way. General William Tecumseh Sherman was in charge of the plans. The route of the parade would be along Pennsylvania Avenue and past the White House. Protocol dictated that a general would ride in front of the division he had commanded.

On the morning of the parade, a hitch developed. General Sherman looked troubled as he approached General Oliver O. Howard. This general's corps had helped gain victories in the Tennessee and Atlanta campaigns. Promoted to command of the Army of Tennessee, he had taken part in Sherman's famous "march to the sea."

"General Howard, you know that you are slated to ride in front of your division."

"Yes, sir."

"Well, I would like to ask a favor."

"Yours to command, sir."

"General _____ who preceded you in command wants to ride at the head of his old division. I know you were in command during the last campaigns. But Howard, I know that you are a Christian and so can afford to be disappointed. Would you step down and allow General _____ to have the honor of leading the troops in the parade."

General Howard was momentarily stunned. He had looked forward to riding with the troops who had served him so loyally and sacrificially. A tremendous *esprit de corps* had developed as they had lived and fought together. Those men would have died for him and for one another. He had lost an arm in the service. Now he was being asked to forfeit his place of honor for another officer who was making an unprecedented and unjustified request.

But General Howard recovered promptly. True to the military dictum, "Your request is my command," he stood erect before his commanding officer and said, "Yes, sir. Since you put it that way, and since I am a Christian, I will do it gladly. General _____ may ride at the head of the division."

Sherman looked at him in relief and admiration, then said, "Howard, I expected that you would agree to do it. Now I want you to ride with me at the head of the whole army."

Contrary to normal human behavior, General Howard did the Christian thing. He had learned that rare humility that comes from adopting the mind of Christ. Taking the low place went against the grain of nature. But Sherman honored him in a way that would never have happened otherwise.

Ten

In Sickness and in Health [13]

Robertson McQuilken was president of Columbia Bible College and Seminary. One of the great joys of his life was to train young people to become effective servants of the Lord Jesus Christ. Toward this goal he labored tirelessly. Under his leadership, the college had a reputation for spiritual and academic excellence.

Then the bottom seemed to fall out of everything. It started when his wife Muriel began to tell the same story over again. Then she lost her ability to read and her art skill. She had to stop all public ministry. It was agonizing for Robertson to watch her "gradually dimming out." Finally, when a doctor asked her to name the four Gospels and she couldn't, the diagnosis was confirmed. She had Alzheimer's disease.

She had been Robertson's devoted companion for many years. Without her he could not have carried on the ministry that had been so fruitful. What would he do? Would he arrange to hire caregivers to attend to her, so he could continue his work at the college and seminary? Or would he resign to give back to her some of the care she had lavished on him for so long?

To his associates the decision was clear. There were many friends who would stand in the gap for him, showering Muriel with Christian love and tenderness. That would free him to continue his leadership at Columbia.

But hadn't he vowed to be with his wife in sickness and in health until death parted them? Now she was in sickness and it was irreversible. Of course, God could perform a miracle in Muriel, but if not, He could perform one in Robertson. So what would he do? Would he keep his vow?

Yes, he would keep his vow. To the consternation of the Christian community, he resigned as President of the college and seminary to nurse Muriel through her mental and physical deterioration. "When the time came, the decision was firm. It took no great calculation. It was a matter of integrity.... This was no grim duty to which I stoically resigned, however. She had, after all, cared for me for almost four decades with marvelous devotion; now it was my turn. And such a partner she was! If I took care of her for 40 years, I would never be out of her debt."

For seventeen years Robertson walked with Muriel on her journey into oblivion. He wrote:

It's midnight now, at least for her, and sometimes I wonder when dawn will break. Even the dread Alzheimer's disease isn't supposed to attack so early and torment so long. Yet, in her silent world Muriel is so content, so lovable. If Jesus took her home, how I would miss her gentle, sweet presence. Yes, there are times when I get irritated, but not often. It doesn't make sense to get angry. And besides, perhaps the Lord has been answering the prayer of my youth to mellow my spirit.

Once, though, I completely lost it. In the days when Muriel could still stand and walk and we had not resorted to diapers, sometimes there were "accidents." I was on my knees beside her, trying to clean up the mess, as she stood by the toilet, confused. It would have been easier if she had not been so insistent on helping. I got more and more frustrated. Suddenly, to make her stand still, I slapped her calf—as if that would do any good. It wasn't a hard slap, but she was startled. I was, too. Never in our forty-four years of marriage had I even as much as touched her in anger or in rebuke of any kind. Never; wasn't even tempted, in fact. But now, when she needed me most....

Sobbing, I pled with her to forgive me—no matter that she didn't understand words any better than she could speak them. So I turned to the Lord to tell Him how sorry I was. It took me days to get over it. Maybe God bottled those tears to quench the fires that might ignite some day.

So Robertson McQuilken relinquished the presidency of a Bible College and Seminary that he had held for twenty-two years, in order to care for his wife as she descended into oblivion.

The story was published in *Christianity Today,* a Christian magazine. Readers fought back tears unashamedly. It led some couples who knew the Lord to renew their marriage vows. Others developed a new appreciation of the sacredness of the marriage relationship. Still others realized they had seen Jesus in the life of Robertson McQuilken.

Eleven

My Captain

A public school teacher in Melrose, Massachusetts, had assigned her pupils to memorize *Invictus* by William Ernest Henley and recite it in class. This poem is generally considered a classic of English literature, and she thought that her students should be familiar with it. It inspires unthinking people by its spirit of power, independence, and bravery. The title of the poem is the Latin for "Unconquered."

Actually *Invictus* is thoroughly infidel. It questions the existence of God and scoffs at Him if He does exist. The author boasts of his own self-sufficiency. He needs no God to determine his fate or to tell him what to do. He defies the Almighty. Here is the poem:

Invictus

Out of the night that covers me,
Black as the pit from pole to pole,
I thank whatever gods may be
For my unconquerable soul.

In the fell clutch of circumstance
I have not winced nor cried aloud;
Under the bludgeonings of chance
My head is bloody but unbowed.

Beyond this place of wrath and tears
Looms but the horror of the shade,
And yet the menace of the years
Finds, and shall find me, unafraid.

It matters not how straight the gate,
How charged with punishment the scroll,
I am the master of my fate.
I am the captain of my soul.

Those words posed a problem for Edith Vail, a Christian girl in the class. To recite this poem publicly in class would be a denial of what she believed. It would be dishonoring to the One whom she acknowledged as her Master and Captain.

In fact, she felt that it would be blasphemy against her Lord and Savior.

There was only one thing to do. She went to the teacher and courteously explained her situation. She was neither combative nor disrespectful. The teacher tried to reason with her. She explained that Edith didn't have to agree with the sentiments of the poem, but she should know it as a great piece of literature. It was useless. Edith had drawn a line in the sand. Her convictions were not negotiable.

The teacher felt that here was a case of real insubordination. She reported Edith to the school administration, but it didn't stop there. Someone reported it to the local papers, and soon it was a *cause celèbre*. It was splashed on the front pages: a student who stubbornly refused to obey her teacher. Edith was compared to Jehovah's Witnesses who refuse to pledge allegiance to the flag. She was obviously a member of a rebellious and possibly anti-American cult.

Christians throughout the area prayed fervently for Edith. Then a believer came to her rescue with a brilliant suggestion. She told her that there is a Christian version of Henley's poem by Dorothy Day. Perhaps the teacher would allow her to recite it in place of the offensive one. And that is what happened. Edith took the Christianized version and showed it to her teacher. Much to her surprise, the teacher agreed.

Edith stood before the class and recited the following:

My Captain

Out of the light that dazzles me,
Bright as the sun from pole to pole,
I thank the God I know to be
For Christ, the Conqueror of my soul.

Since His the sway of circumstance
I would not wince nor cry aloud.
Under that rule which men call chance
My head with joy is humbly bowed.

Beyond this place of sin and tears
That life with Him! And His the aid
That, 'spite the menace of the years,
Keeps, and shall keep me unafraid.

I have no fear though strait the gate,
He cleared from punishment the scroll;
Christ is the Master of my fate,
Christ is the Captain of my soul.

God had made the wrath of man to praise Him. He had vindicated a courageous young believer who was willing to suffer verbal abuse for her loyalty to Christ. He had brought a great many people face to face with the inescapable Christ.

It takes backbone to be true to Jesus when all the world seems to be against you. Edith Vail was one of those who had what it takes.

Twelve

Friend of the Social Reject

Jack Wyrtzen was founder and director of the Word of Life Camp at Schroon Lake, New York. The summer months were crowded with Bible conferences, youth camps, and other activities designed to win the lost to Christ, build believers up in their faith, and strengthen local Christian assemblies. Jack was a spiritual leader and a human dynamo. His days were packed with administrative duties, preparation of messages, meeting with guests, and all other tasks necessary for a smooth-running camp.

One year a Christian with an unpleasant disability came to the adult conference. It was particularly noticeable when he was in the dining room. Before the meal started, someone had to take a newspaper, tuck it in at his chin, and cover his chest and lap with it. You see, when he put food in his mouth, he could swallow only a little of it.

Because the muscles of his mouth were impaired, the rest of the food flowed out and down over the newspaper. There was nothing he could do about it. It was only one of his many disabilities. Yet the pathetic saint relished the Word of God and wanted to attend the conference where he could hear it.

The other guests avoided sitting at the same table. Obviously, it was not a setting conducive to gracious eating. Some would have been repulsed, others would have lost their appetite. As a result, this precious child of God invariably sat alone at a table.

Because of his enormous workload, Jack rarely got to the dining room on time. Usually the guests had already begun to eat, and the place was filled with animated conversation.

When guests saw him finally arrive, they would wave to him excitedly, calling for him to come and sit at their table.

But Jack never did. He went to the table where the forsaken brother was eating alone. It was what the Lord Jesus would have done. In doing it, Jack preached one of his best sermons. Silently he reminded the others that the

Savior condescended to the least, the last, and the lowest—and that we too are called to condescend to people of low estate. We should not aspire to get into the good graces of important people (Romans 12:16, LB) but to associate with the lowly (RSV).

People counted it a status symbol to have Jack sit at their table. After all, he was a radio celebrity, a well-known evangelist, and the director of Word of Life, a growing Christian organization. It meant something to go home and tell their friends that they knew Jack Wyrtzen. But because Jack was a humble believer who lived Christ, the status and the special privilege went to the least-esteemed person in the dining room.

Thirteen

Repaying Hatred with Kindness[14]

You might be tempted to think from the name Cubas that he was a Cuban. But he wasn't. Oscar Cubas was a Honduran, serving the Lord across the border in Nicaragua. He was the first national ever to be commended to full-time service for the Lord from the Honduran assemblies. It was a good commendation. The Lord used him to plant a New Testament assembly in a village called Tauquil.

Oscar was unschooled, just a simple Christian. One of his greatest assets was that he had a profound faith in the Word of God and a deep desire to share the Word with others. In addition to that, he sought to practice what he

69

learned in the Bible, and this meant that he was humble, patient, loving, and kind.

The village of Tauquil, however, was a nest of communists. The sympathies and loyalties of the people were with the Sandinistas. But as more and more people came to Christ and the church grew, the communist grip on the populace weakened. It wasn't because the believers became involved in politics; they didn't. It was just because they were salt and light that their positive moral and spiritual influence began to take effect.

In time Oscar faced a problem—the kind that cheers every true servant of the Lord. As the work grew, the church needed a building. Up to then the saints had met in homes, but that was no longer feasible. The believers' houses were too small. So the assembly bought a piece of property, half of which would hold the chapel and the other half a house for Oscar and his family.

At the time, the Christians didn't realize that their property was adjacent to the land of one of the village's leading communists, Santos. This man was no friend of the evangelicals. No doubt he resented the way that communism had lost some of its power in Tauquil. So he began to harass Oscar. Once he even succeeded in getting him jailed on the ridiculous charge that he had cut down a dead tree. When the authorities investigated and realized how bizarre the charge was, they released Oscar.

Did Oscar try to retaliate? Did he denounce his neighbor? Did he seek to defend himself? No, through all the mistreatment he endured, he was Christlike. He made the villagers marvel at his out-of-this-world behavior. The people of Tauquil weren't like that.

When the chapel was finished, Oscar began building his house. It was just across the fence from Santos's. The kitchen was the room of the house closest to Santos's house. Aha! This gave the unhappy neighbor a chance to do his worst. He built a new outdoor latrine close to the fence, where the stench would waft into the Cubas's kitchen, enough to spoil any meal.

Oscar said nothing. He always greeted Santos with friendliness and respect. There was no thought of getting even. In his simple faith, he believed that the battle was God's. He was content to stand still and see the salvation of the Lord.

The latrine had not been a masterpiece of engineering. One day when Santos was using it, the whole thing collapsed—here we will draw a kindly veil over the rest of this inelegant scenario. The humiliated man realized that he had been fighting against God and he was losing badly. Like Saul of Tarsus he was kicking against the goads. He certainly didn't want a repeat of that day's experience.

So now we come to the good news. The sordid episode had a happy ending. It was the means of bringing Santos to Christ. The one who shared this story with us said, "The wonderful thing is that when Santos surrendered to the Lord, he gave himself fully to him. He is now a devoted Christian brother in full fellowship in the little assembly and actively reaching out to others."

The psalmist said, *"The Lord takes pleasure in His people"* (Psalm 149:4). It's easy to see how He can take pleasure in a man like Oscar Cubas. This homespun believer exemplified Christ. He endured patiently when suffering for well doing. He chose to be wronged rather than to stand up for his rights. He prayed for those who persecuted him and let the Lord do the rest. He did not retaliate.

Having said that, let's ask why it is that Christians are to be non-retaliatory. The reason is that we lose our credibility as the alternative society if we behave exactly as other people do. Part of our witness to Christ and His saving grace is an attitude of meekness. In other words, the entire mission of the church, the witness of the gospel, is affected if Christians give in to retaliation or revenge.[15]

Fourteen

He Turned the Other Cheek[16]

This is a story that seems to surface every time a war breaks out and men and women are called up for military service. It is impossible to know the original version. No doubt, it has occurred many times.

Dr. J. Stuart Holden, a British preacher, gave a version of the story which we can know is authentic because it was told to him directly by one of the participants.

At the end of WWII, Holden met a British sergeant in Egypt who was an outstanding Christian. When Holden asked him how he had come to faith in the Lord Jesus, the sergeant explained that before coming to Egypt, he was stationed in Malta. There was a private in his company who was a believer who was not ashamed to witness to the other men. They took delight in harassing him, but it didn't seem to bother him.

The sergeant said, "One night we all came to the barracks, very wet from the rains, and very tired. Before crawling into his bunk, this private got down on his knees and prayed. I sure let him have it! My boots were heavy with mud, and I hit him on one side of the face with one of the boots. Then I took the other boot and slung it at the other side of his face. He just kept on praying."

"The next morning," the sergeant continued, "I found those boots by the side of my bunk, beautifully polished. That was the private's response to my cruelty. It broke my heart. That very day I was saved."

The private's reaction to the sergeant's persecution was a vivid portrayal of the Savior's words, *"To him who strikes you on the one cheek, offer the other also"* (Luke 6:29). He had not followed his Master in vain.

I would just add a word of caution. We should not suppose that physical abuse always follows a vibrant testimony for Christ in the armed forces. More often, I think, worldly men and women have respect for a believer who has convictions and is willing to stand up for them. Even if one soldier acts offensively toward a Christian, other non-believers are often quick to come to his defense. The Lord suits the wind to the shorn lamb. He doesn't give us more than we are able to bear at any particular time.

Fifteen

The Warmest Fire

In his book *From Grace to Glory*,[17] Murdoch Campbell tells of a godly minister in the north of Scotland whose wife did not share his deep spirituality. Apparently she did not have the same love for the Lord or for His Word. One day when he was sitting by the fire, reading the Bible, she entered the room in a fit of anger. She grabbed the Book out of his hands and threw it in the fire.

How should a Christian respond to such sacrilege and anger? Should he rebuke her sternly for such ungodly behavior? Or should he use it as an occasion to show a Christlike spirit?

The minister chose the latter. He looked at her and said quietly, "I don't think I've ever sat by a warmer fire." Here was a classic illustration of the proverb, *"A soft answer turns away wrath"* (Proverbs 15:1). Mr. Campbell writes, "It was an answer that turned away her wrath and marked the beginning of a new and gracious life. His Jezebel became a Lydia. The thorn became a lily."

But something must be quickly added to make the picture complete. Christian women have more often been the victims than the assailants.

Linda is an example.[18] Before she was saved, she married a fellow named Tony. She thought he was good looking and charming.

But by the time their first child was born and she had become a believer, she knew that Tony was a loser. She shouldn't have judged by appearance. He was allergic to work and a stranger to responsible living. He was a boozer and a womanizer. Sometimes he would leave for months, then return home as if nothing had happened, and again live with Linda as her husband. By the time the next baby was born, he would take off again, leaving Linda to provide for the family.

As a godly wife, Linda sought to follow the pattern described in 1 Peter 3:1-2:

Likewise you wives, be submissive to your own husbands, that even if some do not obey the Word, they, without a word, may be won by the conduct of their wives, when they observe your chaste conduct accompanied by fear.

Instead of retaliating or nagging, Linda tried to win her husband through a life of righteousness and by behavior that comes from another world. Books could be written of similar women who obeyed Peter's counsel and lived to see their husbands come to Christ.

Sixteen

Love Your Enemies

There is no question that Jesus said, *"Love your enemies"* (Luke 6:27), but did He mean it literally? Or was He merely holding this up as an ideal toward which we should strive? It's so unnatural to love one's foes. Why should we love them when they will probably only increase their hostility? It seems impossible to love those who hate us. So in reading this command of our Lord, we tend to explain it away in order to raise our comfort level.

Yet deep in our hearts we know that the Lord Jesus meant what He said. What we forget is that when He commands something, He gives us the power to obey that command. Humanly speaking, it is impossible to love our enemies. That is true of the Christian life in general. It can be lived only by the power of the indwelling Holy Spirit.

Our tendency to dull the sharp edge of the Savior's words ends when we see the command obeyed by another believer. Many verses of Scripture come alive to us when we see them in action. You can't argue against a fact. Show me a Christian who actually does love his enemy and I am convinced.

That happened to me. I saw Luke 6:27 fleshed out in a human life. It was in the life of a man named Theo McCully. He was the father of Ed McCully, one of the five martyrs of Ecuador, and the Board Chairman of the Bible School where I was an administrator.

One night, he and I met to discuss some current affairs of the school and some of the decisions we faced. Mr. McCully never told me what to do. He always said, "Let's pray about it." So at the close of the evening, we got down on our knees and prayed at length concerning the school.

As he neared the end of his prayer, his mind went south to the shores of the Curaray River in Ecuador where Stone Age Indians had speared his missionary son to death. Ed had been an ideal son. His father once told me that Ed had never caused his parents an anxious moment. Now Theo prayed, "Lord, let me live long enough to see those fellows saved who killed our boys, so I can throw my arms around them and tell them I love them, because they love my Christ."

When we rose, tears were zigzagging down his cheeks. It was a sacred moment, one that can never be recaptured. Here was a man who truly loved the guilty murderers of his beloved son, a son who had abandoned a legal career to bring the gospel to the Auca (subsequently known as Waorani) Indians.

Not surprisingly, it was a prayer that reached the throne of God. Missionaries finally made successful contact with the Waoranis and in time were able to lead several of the killers to Christ. Theo's prayer was answered. He went to Ecuador, lovingly embraced the new believers, and told them he loved them because his Savior was now their Savior, too.

Yes, Jesus meant what He said. We should love our enemies. When we do, we impact the world. We show other believers practical ways to carry out this command. We bring difficult sayings of Jesus to life. And, we give a true representation of what the Lord Jesus is like. He loved us—His enemies—enough to die for us.

Seventeen

To Forgive is Divine[19]

The Ten Booms were a godly Christian family in Holland. During the Second World War their home was a haven for Jewish people who were trying to hide from the Nazis. If the Jews were discovered, it meant the concentration camp, unspeakable suffering, and usually death. To hide Jews at that time meant the concentration camp also.

After successfully sheltering Jews for a long time, the Ten Booms were caught. The father and two daughters, Corrie and Betsie, were carted off to the Ravensbruck camp, a place of indescribable cruelty and inhuman torture. Eventually Mr. Ten Boom and then Betsie died. Corrie survived and was released when the war was over.

After peace had been declared, Corrie went to Germany

and was speaking one night in the basement hall of a church building. Among other things she spoke of the marvel that when we confess our sins, the Lord casts them in the deepest sea and erects a sign that says, "No fishing."

At the close of the service the people walked out quietly, but one man worked his way down to the front where Corrie was standing. He was wearing a blue uniform and holding a visored cap with a skull and cross bones. Corrie recognized him. He had been a guard at Ravensbruck.

When he reached Corrie, he held out his hand and said, "A fine message, Fräulein. How good it is to know that, as you say, all our sins are at the bottom of the sea."

Memories of his cruelty flashed before her and her blood boiled.

"You mentioned Ravensbruck," he continued. "I was a guard there. But since that time, I have become a Christian. I know that God has forgiven me for the cruel things I did there, but I would like to hear it from your lips as well, Fräulein. Will you forgive me?"

Her knee-jerk reaction would understandably have been

bitter and unforgiving. She could have rehearsed the savagery committed against the Jews and the inhumane treatment of her own family until her gastric juices turned to sulfuric acid.

Corrie stood there transfixed. It seemed like hours, though it was only a few seconds, before she could reply. Finally she was able to pull her hand out of her coat pocket and thrust it into the hand of the ex-guard. "If God has forgiven me, how can I do less than forgive you? I forgive you, brother, with all my heart."

"For a long moment they grasped each other's hands, the former guard and the former prisoner, now made one in Christ."

Whenever I think of Christlike behavior, my mind inevitably goes to the Ten Boom family. Such sorrow. Such suffering. Such humiliation. Yet, through it all, they had the mind of Christ—thinking of others, not of themselves. They did not become bitter or cynical, nor did they complain against God. Through it all, they witnessed to the love and grace of the Lord Jesus and forgave those who put them through the fires of Nazi brutality.

Eighteen

Where There's a Will...[20]

Grandma Phillips often rejoiced that she, her two sons and their wives lived in happy fellowship. They were all believers and so were their children. The older son, Scott, and his wife, Sarah, lived in the same town as Gram and visited her regularly, making sure she was eating well and was able to do her housekeeping. The other son, Ron, and his wife, Rose, were also able to visit regularly although they lived twenty miles away. Both sons had good positions and were financially secure. The entire family met to celebrate Thanksgiving and Christmas and also for occasional cookouts.

Then Grandma died suddenly of a coronary. They found her sitting in her rocking chair, the open Bible on her lap. She didn't leave much. There was the modest house where she and her late husband had raised the boys. She had a few stocks, like AT&T, General Electric, and General Motors. There was a savings account of about $10,000, and her collection of bone china teacups. She had not left a last will and testament, thinking that the boys would be able to distribute things amicably.

That is not how it happened. Rose suddenly became ultra-possessive. Ron felt that he had no alternative but to be loyal to his wife. For him it was a case of peace at any price. A family that had lived happily for many years now was wracked by greed. Trivial things like bone china cups became the cause of controversy. Scott and Sarah did their best to be conciliatory, but they met with animosity.

As Scott and Sarah prayed fervently for a peaceful solution, Scott remembered the story of Abram and Lot. When these two men left Egypt and came to Canaan, they found that there wasn't sufficient pasture for their herds. Strife broke out between their herdsmen. The situation was serious. Then Abram said to Lot:

> Please let there be no strife between you and me, and between my herdsmen and your herdsmen; for we are brethren.
> Is not the whole land before you? Please separate from me.

If you take the left, then I will go to the right; or, if you go to the right, then I will go to the left (Genesis 13:8-9).

Lot chose the well-watered plain of Jordan where the pasture was rich, and he dwelt in the city of Sodom. Abram chose the land of Canaan.

As Scott shared this with Sarah, they came to a momentous decision. They would let Ron and Rose take the entire estate if they so desired. To preserve the family unity was more important than to fight over material items.

Ron and Rose were nonplussed. Because they hadn't expected this, they were too ashamed to take everything. Rose satisfied herself with some costume jewelry, the china, and other trifles. Then they suggested that the remaining proceeds be divided equally. It was a peaceful solution to a potentially alienating situation.

It doesn't always happen that way. The saying often comes true, "Where there's a will, there's a lot of relatives." People who are normally generous and peaceful will argue and break fellowship over things that are faded and jaded.

God's way is the best way. Abram enriched himself by

yielding his property rights to Lot. Lot impoverished himself by choosing pasture land near Sodom.

Nineteen

Enduring Shame and Spitting

Dick Faulkner was serving as song leader for a church group on a tour of New Testament sites. They had come to the Isle of Patmos in the Aegean Sea. Their guide had taken them into the cave where the apostle John is said to have written the Book of Revelation. When they emerged, they climbed a nearby hillside where the host gave a message about John's imprisonment by the Emperor Domitian. When he finished, he asked Dick to sing.

Dick was holding a tape recorder with large speakers that would amplify his voice. He began to sing Don Wyrtzen's rendition of Revelation 5:12:

Worthy is the Lamb that was slain,

Worthy is the Lamb that was slain,
Worthy is the Lamb that was slain, to receive:
Power and riches and wisdom and strength,
Honor and glory and blessing!
Worthy is the Lamb,
Worthy is the Lamb,
Worthy is the Lamb that was slain,
Worthy is the Lamb.

The message went out over the rocky landscape of Patmos.

Before Dick had finished, another tour bus arrived. Most of the people passed by, but a small, dark-skinned woman came close to Dick and spat at him. Her aim was good. She hit the target, but that did not stop the song. Dick went right on until the final "Worthy is the Lamb."

Some of the Christian tour party felt that something should be said or done to the offender for this gross insult, but Dick did not share their sentiment. After all, men covered our Lord's face with shame and with spitting, and He did not fight back. He was mocked and insulted and spat upon, but He did not return tit for tat. When men spat upon the Lord Jesus, it was the creatures saying to the Creator, "This is what we think of You."

When the Creator died on the Cross, He was saying to His creatures, "This is how much I love you."

We are called to have His spirit. *"Beloved, do not avenge yourselves, but rather give place to wrath; for it is written, 'Vengeance is Mine, I will repay,' says the Lord"* (Romans 12:19). We are living in the acceptable year of the Lord, and not in the day of vengeance of our God.

Twenty
The Jewish Junk Dealer

Back in the days when people saved newspapers, rags, and metals, they would occasionally hear a junk dealer driving down the street and crying out some readily identifiable notice of his presence.

One day H. A. Ironside heard the familiar call, hurried out to the porch, and told the man to come to the cellar. This particular junk dealer was a Jew, a people for whom Ironside had great affection because his Savior was also Jewish.

In the cellar there was quite a stash of newspapers, and a fairly large pile of pipes and other metals.

Ironside decided to engage in a friendly round of bargaining, trying to get as much as possible. Not that he really cared. The important thing was to get the junk out of the basement.

So he extolled the great value of his hoard of castaways. But the dealer was on to his trick, so he played the game magnificently—and won. He handed a trifling sum to Ironside and began to cart off his loot.

As he was leaving with the last load, Dr. Ironside called him back, pressed some money into his hand, and said, "Here. I want to give you this in the name of Jesus."

The junk man was stunned for a moment. Then he walked away, muttering, "No one ever gave me anything in the name of Jesus before."

Isn't that act of kindness by Dr. Ironside something like the Lord Jesus would have done?

Twenty-One

The Emperor's Gladiators

It was some time after the resurrection of Christ, when the infamous Nero was in power. He had an elite division of soldiers who were chosen because of their athletic prowess. They were known as the Emperor's gladiators. Physically, these men were outstanding specimens of humanity. They were handsome, muscular, and well proportioned—the cream of Roman manhood.

When they marched into the Coliseum, they sang, "We are the Emperor's wrestlers. We wrestle for you, O king. Whether to live or to die, it's all for your glory." Then they would put on a wrestling match for Nero.

The time came when they were sent north to battle Germanic tribes. It was also the time when a decree went out to suppress the Christian faith. Nero sent specific orders to weed out any Christians who might be in the army. "Weed out" was a euphemism for destroy.

In the dead of winter, General Vespasian lined up his troops, including the gladiators. He barked out, "It has come to my attention that some of you might have embraced this new superstition called Christianity. I doubt that it is true. You're too smart for that. But if any of you are Christians, I want you to step forward." To his surprise, forty gladiators took the step that could spell death.

The general dismissed all the other troops and for the rest of the day tried to talk the forty out of their faith. "Think of your families. Think of your fellow soldiers. Think of what you're losing. Think of the consequences if you don't renounce Christianity." The forty believers were impervious to his appeals and threats.

When Vespasian saw that further efforts were futile, he assembled his army and gave one last opportunity to recant. "I order any Christians in this army to take a step forward." Forty of the elite men stepped forward without hesitation. He could have ordered the execution squad to kill them on the spot but he had another plan.

When darkness fell, his troops took them out on a frozen lake, undressed them, and left them there in the bitter cold to die of exposure. Vespasian said to the naked men,

"If you come to your senses and will renounce your faith, then walk back to the shore. There will be fires all around the lake as well as warm clothes and food."

Through the night, the other soldiers, who were posted around the lake, peered into the darkness, trying to see what was happening. They couldn't see but every once in a while they heard the men singing, "We are Christ's forty wrestlers. We wrestle for You. O King! To live or die, it is for Your glory."

At dawn they saw one pathetic figure painfully making his way across the ice to one of the bonfires. The soldiers rushed out to meet him, wrapped him in blankets, and hurried him to the warmth of the fire. The man had renounced his faith.

Then across the icy lake they heard a song: "We are Christ's thirty-nine wrestlers. We wrestle for You, O King. To live or die, it is for Your glory."

Vespasian had arrived in time to see the one deserter and to hear the thirty-nine victors. His resolve was firm. He took off his armor and walked out to die with the thirty-nine men who would rather die than deny their Lord.

Twenty-Two

The First Commandment with Promise

Reuben Torrey, American evangelist and Biblical scholar, used to tell of a widowed mother in Georgia who had an only son. They lived below the poverty level but she was able to make ends meet by taking in washing. She didn't complain. She accepted it as from the Lord.

The son was exceptionally brilliant. In fact, he was the top student in the graduating class at high school. Apart from the Lord, he was the bright spot in his mother's life.

Because of his academic record, he was chosen to deliver the valedictory message at the Commencement exercises. He would also be presented with a gold medal for excellence in one of his subjects.

When the day for graduation arrived, he noticed that his mother was not making preparations to attend. He said to her, "Mother, this is Commencement Day. It's the day I graduate. Why aren't you getting ready?"

"Oh," she said rather wearily, "I'm not going. I don't have any decent clothes to wear. All the prominent people of the town will be there, dressed in their finery. You would be ashamed of your old mother in her faded cotton dress."

His eyes beamed with admiration for her. "Mother," he said, "Don't say that. I will never be ashamed of you. Never! I owe everything I have in the world to you, and I won't go unless you do." He persisted until she agreed, then helped her dress to look her best.

They started down the street arm in arm. Once inside the high school auditorium, he escorted her to one of the best seats at the front. And there she sat in her freshly ironed cotton dress among prominent townspeople in their elegant attire.

When his time came, he delivered the valedictory address without a fluff. There was considerable applause. Then the principal honored him with the gold medal. No sooner had he received it than he walked down off the platform, made his way to where his mother was sitting, pinned the gold medal on her dress, and said, "Here, Mother, this belongs to you. You are the one who earned it." This time the applause was thunderous. The audience rose to their feet and tears streamed down the cheeks of many.

That son gave a living example of obedience to Ephesians 6:2: *"Honor your father and mother."* Whenever Dr. Torrey told the story, he made an additional application. He would say, "Never be ashamed of the Lord Jesus. You owe everything to Him. Stand up and confess Him. The martyrs were not ashamed. Onesiphorus was not ashamed of Paul (2 Timothy 1:16). Paul was not ashamed of the gospel (Romans 1:16) or of the One in whom he had believed (2 Timothy 1:12). We should never be ashamed of Christ."

Twenty-Three

The God Who Loves[21]

In the history of Christian missions, Gladys Aylward will always be known as "The Little Woman." But what she lacked in physical stature, she more than made up in spiritual achievement. This intrepid missionary had a simple faith in the Lord and displayed a resolute fearlessness, fortitude, and endurance in serving Him. As a result, she saw marvelous answers to prayer, amazing converging of circumstances, and an astonishing number of open doors for the gospel in China.

Once she was staying in a home with student refugees who had fled from the Japanese invaders. These young people were praying for an area in the northwest. For various reasons they were not free to go, so Gladys concluded that the Lord wanted her to do it. She set out, depending on guides to accompany her from one village to another. When she reached Tsin Tsui, the villagers tried to dissuade her from going farther. They said, "This is the end. There's nothing further." But Gladys countered, "The world doesn't end just like that. I must go on. It is what I have come for."

When a Chinese Christian doctor named Huang saw that she was determined, he offered to accompany her for five days. The five days stretched on to ten, as they spoke to everyone they met about Jesus. No one had ever heard of Him. On day eleven, they trekked through a barren area without any sign of human habitation. There was no place to sleep, no food to eat. It was time to pray. Gladys began: "Dear God, have mercy on us. You can see what a plight we are in. Give us food and shelter for the night." She felt rebuked that her prayer was all about her and the doctor.

Then Dr. Huang prayed: "O God, send us the one You want us to tell about Jesus. We have witnessed to no one today, but You have sent us here for some special purpose. Show us where to find the man You intend to bless." This man was concerned only with the work of the Lord.

Gladys decided that they should sing a chorus, so the words and melody wafted out in the clear mountain air.

Soon Dr. Huang spotted a man in the distance, jumped

up, and dashed off to meet him. The doctor yelled for
Miss Aylward to come, but she didn't want to climb the
steep, rugged mountain and leave their bundles unguard-
ed. So he returned and finally persuaded her to come. She
need not worry about their baggage; there was no one to
steal it.

When they reached the man, she was surprised to learn
that he was a Tibetan lama or monk. In spite of the fact
that lamas were not supposed to have anything to do with
women, this one invited Huang and Gladys to come and
spend the night at the lamasery. When the priest saw that
she was hesitating, he said, "We have waited long for you
to tell us about the God who loves." The little woman was
shocked. How could they know that there is a God who
loves? What contact could such secluded people have had
with missionaries or with anyone else from the outside
world?

After the lamas had provided cushions, water for washing, and delicious food, two of them appeared at Gladys's
door and asked her to come with them. Others brought
Dr. Huang to the same place, a room with 500 monks sitting on hassocks. All this puzzled Gladys, but the good
doctor must have understood the purpose of their gather-
ing so he told her to begin by singing a chorus. When she

finished, he told about the Savior's birth at Bethlehem and continued to the Savior's death and resurrection.

Miss Aylward sang again, then talked; sang again, then Dr. Huang talked, sang again, then talked. Finally she excused herself and went to her room. She was exhausted. But her work was not finished. Two lamas appeared at her door and asked her to tell them more. When they left, two more came, and this went on all night. They seemed to be especially interested in the God who loves.

After five days of unhindered evangelism, Miss Aylward was invited for a meeting with the head lama. To her relief, she learned that he could speak Mandarin, which she understood perfectly. She asked why he had allowed a foreign woman to come into the lamasery and speak to the priests. He then recounted this remarkable story:

Each year the lamas collect and sell a licorice herb that grows on the mountains. One year as they came to a village, they heard a man holding a tract and calling out, "Who wants one? Salvation is free and for nothing. He who gets salvation lives forever. If you want to learn more, come to the gospel hall."

They took the tract back to the lamasery and tacked it to

the wall. On it John 3:16 was quoted: *"For God so loved the world that He gave His only begotten Son, that whosoever believeth on Him should not perish but have everlasting life."* This was a constant reminder to them that there is a God who loves.

For five years they took the herbs to market, each time asking where "the God who loves" lived. Finally in Len Chow a man directed them to the China Inland Mission compound where a missionary explained the way of salvation and gave them a copy of the Gospels. As they studied it, they came to Mark 16:15: *"Go ye into all the world and preach the gospel to every creature."* From this they concluded that eventually someone would come to them with the gospel. They decided that when God sent a messenger, they should be ready to receive him.

They waited for another three years. Then two monks, working out on the mountains, heard someone singing. They said, "Only people who know God will sing." When one man came down the mountain to meet Gladys and Dr. Huang, the other returned to the lamasery, alerting his fellow lamas to prepare for the long-expected guests.

That was why the two Christians were received so warmly and with such hungry hearts.

Were any of the lamas converted? Gladys Aylward left without knowing. All she knew was that the Lord had led her and Dr. Huang to them by a series of divine appointments, and she was content to leave the result with Him. It is doubtful that He would have arranged such intricate circumstances only to be frustrated at last.

The little woman imitated the Lord Jesus by her fresh, wholesome faith, by her obedience to His promptings, and by her faithful confession of Him before others. She saw the gears of her life meshing. Her service sparkled with the supernatural. When she touched other lives, something happened for God.

Twenty-Four

Incredible Grace[22]

I am going to assign fictitious names to this couple for reasons that will become clear as the story progresses. Ernie was an officer in the U. S. Army, stationed at a large base in the United States. Elise was content to forego an outside career; she felt that her calling was to stay at home and raise their two children. Apart from the usual minor disagreements, theirs was a happy marriage.

Then Ernie was transferred to Japan. It was at a time when families were not free to accompany the parent. But this family kept in close touch by mail. It was always a high spot in the week when a letter arrived from Daddy. The children would sit on the floor near Mother while she read the letter to them. The news became the subject of discussion for the rest of the day. It seemed that Daddy was not far away.

So it was a cause of alarm when a week passed without a letter. Elise had a vivid imagination. She pictured Ernie ill, or in an accident, or off on some dangerous, secret mission. Two weeks passed, and no letter. If there had been an accident or illness, she would have been notified by now. Three weeks and still no mail. Four. Finally a letter arrived, and the blow fell. Elise's recent fears had become reality. It was incredible. What had she done to deserve this? She was devastated, too crushed to share it with the children.

Finally one of the kids asked, "Mommy, what's wrong? Has something happened to Daddy? What did he say in the letter?"

It was torture to tell them that their father had fallen in love with another woman. She saw the look of shock on their faces. They obviously couldn't take it all in at the time. But they did realize that their Daddy wouldn't be coming back to them anymore. Finally, one of them said, "Mommy, can I ask you something? Just because Daddy doesn't love us anymore, does that mean we can't love him?"

Elise was struck by the question. It reminded her of Psalm 8:2: *"Out of the mouth of babes and nursing infants You have ordained strength. "* In her desolation and sorrow, the idea had never occurred to her. After wrestling with the question, she replied, "No, we're allowed to love him." But there was a lump in her throat when she said it. Her little son said, "Well, will you write him and ask him to please keep writing to us because we still want to love him?" This meant that letters would perhaps still come from him.

As they did, the details of his unfaithfulness unfolded. He had fallen in love with his fifteen-year-old servant girl. Subsequently, he had several children from that marriage. Elise still had a hard time in believing what had happened. But she was still not shockproof. Another outrage was in the wings.

It was a letter from Ernie. "Dear Elise: I am sorry to be writing like this to you, but I have been diagnosed with cancer, and do not have long to live. I have forfeited my pension, and we are living on a shoestring. After I die, would you be willing to send some money to help my family?"

After reading it, Elise said to herself, "Well, now I've heard everything." She couldn't believe his gall and impenitence. Not a word of apology. No confession or

117

request for forgiveness. It was incomprehensible.

But on more sober reflection, she remembered what her son had asked, "Mommy, just because Daddy doesn't love us anymore, does that mean we can't love him?" So she wrote back and explained that although she would not be able to send money, there was something she would do. She wrote, "I'll tell you what I'll do. Why don't you arrange to have them come to America after you've passed away? They can stay in this home and I'll teach them how to be self-supporting."

And that's what happened. Elise later explained, "I had two choices. I could look back over the past and curse that man for what he did to me, or I could thank God for giving me the privilege of shining His light in a very dark tunnel in this world."

No doubt, shining His light in a very dark tunnel included sharing the gospel with this adopted family so that they too could become lights for the Lord.

Archbishop Temple was right when he said, "To return evil for good is devilish. To return good for good is human. To return good for evil is divine."

Twenty-Five

He Loved the Poor[23]

John Nelson Darby was no sycophant; he did not cozy up to the rich and famous. That was somewhat out of character because he had been brought up in a wealthy home and in a class-conscious society. It would have been natural for him to favor the fellowship of the upper class and to prefer accommodations where his comfort would be maximized.

But no, he loved the poor and let the fact be known in unconventional ways that left no doubt in people's minds. One time when he was ministering the Word on the Continent, he arrived by train at a town where he was scheduled to be for several days of meetings. The large crowd of Christians who gathered at the station to meet him included some blue-blooded ladies who vied for the honor of being hostess to the distinguished preacher. If he had gone to their palatial homes, he would have had the ultimate in food and furnishings. They in turn would have been able to boast to their family and friends that they had entertained the illustrious Mr. Darby.

J. N. D. looked over the crowd and took in the situation. He asked those who seemed to be leaders, "Who generally takes care of the preachers who come to town?" They pointed to an inconspicuous man, obviously of modest means, standing at the back of the crowd. Darby went to the man and asked if he could stay at his house. The unimposing brother was delighted, and hurried to collect Darby's suitcase. One of J. N. D.'s biographers wrote, "And so the entertainer of obscure itinerants became the host of the great man himself."

Darby explained his love for the poor.

> Christ loved the poor; ever since I have been converted, so
> have I. Let those who like society better, have it. If I ever get
> into it, and it has crossed my path in London, I return sick
> at heart. I go to the poor; I find the same evil nature as in
> the rich, but I find this difference: the rich, and those who
> keep their comforts and their society, judge and measure
> how much of Christ they can take and keep without com-
> mitting themselves; the poor [measure] how much of Christ

they can have to comfort them in their sorrows.

It is interesting that in His training of the seventy disciples, Christ brought up the subject of hospitality.

But whatever house you enter, first say, "Peace to this house." And if a son of peace is there, your peace will rest on it; if not, it will return to you. And remain in the same house....Do not go from house to house" (Luke 10:5-7).

Here He was teaching that they should accept the hospitality that was offered to them by a person who was open to the message of peace. But they should not leave one house for another in hopes of more comfortable lodging and better food.

This is not exactly the same situation that Darby faced. Here they should accept what was offered to them. There he forthrightly asked to live with the poor. But the principle is the same. They should not shop around for the most luxurious housing. Notice the commands, *"Remain in the same house....Do not go from house to house."*

Twenty-Six

Bare Feet in Church[24]

Writing in *Our Daily Bread*, Dennis DeHaan tells of a minor crisis that erupted in an upscale, suburban church. One Sunday, a young Christian from a nearby college walked in barefooted, wearing a t-shirt and jeans. The congregation shifted around uneasily. Doesn't he know that you don't attend church in bare feet? Doesn't he see that the men are supposed to wear a suit and a dress shirt?

Well, the pews were so full that Bill had to go all the way down to the front. There were no empty seats there, so he sat on the floor, squarely in front of the pulpit. No one had ever done this before. It was a day of broken traditions, and it didn't sit well with some of the parishioners.

Then an elderly, arthritic senior broke another tradition. Taking his cane, he made his way to the front. What was going to happen now? Dropping his cane, he lowered himself painfully and sat beside young Bill. He didn't want this young fellow to feel alone and unwanted.

It reminds me of a similar incident that took place at a chapel not far from where I live. It was in the days of the hippies, the flower children, the love generation. A new believer showed up at the evening's Lord's Supper in bare feet. Not many paid attention to it, but one elderly saint felt obligated to straighten him out at the close of the meeting. An elder saw what was happening, and so, when she had finished her lecture, he went over, put his arm around the young fellow, and said, "Never mind. I think they're beautiful." He replied, "Well, they're original."

Hats off to the arthritic senior and the compassionate elder. And hats off to all believers who can see beyond the externals and detect a heart that loves the Lord Jesus. Criticism will only drive them away. Love will help them grow. The Christlike spirit says, *"Permit them to come to Me."*

Twenty-Seven

Shot Down Over the Amazon

Jim and Roni Bowers had been to the consulate in Letitia, Colombia to get a Peruvian residency visa for their newly adopted daughter Charity (seven months). Now they were flying back to their houseboat in Iquitos, Peru, in their mission's Cessna floatplane. The pilot was their missionary colleague and close friend, Kevin Donaldson. Peering out one of the back windows was Cory Bowers (seven), fascinated by the lush Peruvian landscape.

Soon Kevin and Jim noticed that a Peruvian air force fighter was tailing them. They didn't see that there was another jet with a CIA crew that was cooperating with the fighter, part of a massive drive to stop the flow of drugs in that area. The CIA claims that they advised the Peruvian pilot to investigate carefully before firing on the Cessna, but it was too late.

One bullet ripped through Roni's back, then into Charity's head, who was in Roni's lap. They both died instantly. Another bullet shattered the pilot's right leg. And others punctured the fuel tank, setting the plane on fire. Jim was able to extinguish the cabin fire and Kevin miraculously settled the burning plane on its pontoons in a tributary of the Amazon. The fighter continued to fire on the missionaries, even after the plane was down.

By this time the plane was in flames, yet Jim was able to retrieve the bodies of his wife and daughter and get them out into the water. He felt quite cool in spite of the raging inferno.

Kevin swam with Cory on his back while Jim swam away from the burning plane, pulling the bodies of Roni and Charity. He held them face down so that Cory would not see the faces of his dead mother and sister. When the plane sank enough to extinguish the fire, Kevin and Jim were able to swim back and cling to one of the floats on the plane.

Soon some nationals came to their aid in a motorized canoe.

The Peruvian authorities and the CIA surveillance crew

immediately blamed one another for the senseless killing and the shootdown. In striking contrast was the Christlike attitude of Jim Bowers, Kevin Donaldson, and the mission headquarters in the U. S. There was no pointing the finger of blame, no threat of lawsuits. Instead there were repeated testimonies of faith in the Lord and of submission to Him.

Bowers later said, "Our attitude toward those responsible is one of forgiveness. Is that not amazing? It shouldn't be amazing to us Christians…. I've been praying for them (the pilots). I've talked to their supervisor about that. He's very interested in knowing more about the Lord. I've called him from here (home). So everything's going well in that regard. No hard feelings."

In spite of his shattering loss, he said, "Both Cory and I are experiencing inexplicable peace." *Newsweek* magazine commented, "Few had such single-minded faith."

At the memorial service for his devoted wife and baby daughter, Jim was able to trace the sunshine through the rain. He saw God's hand in a series of miracles that took place that heartbreaking day.

Of the fusillade of bullets that penetrated the cabin, not

one hit Cory or himself despite the fact that one coming from behind him made a hole in the windshield right in front of where he was sitting.

The fire extinguisher worked exceptionally well for a little while, contrary to his usual experience with them. He was surprised.

If the bullet that killed Roni and Charity had not stopped where it did, it probably would have killed the pilot, and in that case all the occupants of the plane would have perished.

Neither Cory nor he were terrified. There was no screaming or yelling. They experienced the peace of Christ that passes knowledge. And they were able to think clearly and to react quickly.

A pilot needs the use of his legs to land a Cessna. Despite Kevin's serious leg injury, he was still able to bring the plane safely onto the river, although it was a long way off when the plane was first shot. Kevin knows it was the Lord who piloted the plane on to the water.

Jim had just enough strength to get the bodies of Roni and Charity out of the aircraft in spite of the raging flames. He marvels that he did not feel the heat of the fire. It was cool. His experience mirrors that of the three Hebrews in the fiery furnace (Daniel 3:27).

When the plane sank enough to extinguish the flames, Kevin, Cory, and Jim were able to grab one of the pontoons and stay afloat.

A motorized canoe came just when Kevin and Jim were running out of strength to stay afloat with Cory and the two bodies.

They were shot down over a town where Jim knew some of the people. These people witnessed what had happened and had a radio to call for help. This particular radio worked.

When Jim used the radio to call Kevin's wife, she was at home. A pilot friend was on hand, ready to fly to get Kevin and take him for medical assistance.

Cory and Jim experienced a peace that is supernatural, obviously in answer to the prayers of God's people. Some people told Jim that it wouldn't last, but he was confident that it would.

One final miracle. The Bowers, the Donaldsons and all

the Christians who were involved in any way had a forgiving attitude toward those who were responsible for the tragedy. It was the love of God shed abroad in their hearts.

Roni and Charity did not die in vain. Their passing has stirred a new interest in missionary work. People are challenged to go in answer to the Great Commission. Jim said, "I think He wanted to wake up sleeping Christians, including myself, and maybe most of all, to wake up those who have no interest or little interest in God."

Finally, God extended Cory's life, giving him a further opportunity to receive Jesus Christ as his Lord and Savior.

As time goes on, it becomes more and more clear that the world has seen a vivid display of the fact that Christians are different. A *Prime Time* news magazine gave a fairly complete account of the shootdown on May 24, 2001. On that program Diane Sawyer called the incident "a story of human love, and suffering, and a kind of absolute faith most of us can only view from afar."

Twenty-Eight

Louise and the Sanitary Engineer[25]

Louise is the consummate homemaker. She fits the biblical profile of a Christian wife and mother. One of her great joys is to raise her seven children for God. Another is to support her husband as he travels widely and labors tirelessly for the Lord Jesus. Here is an example. Once when he was speaking at a conference in New Jersey, he remembered that it was her birthday. He called and expressed his regret that he could not be with her and give her a present. Without hesitation she said, "You couldn't give me a better present than being where God wants you to be, doing what He wants you to do."

There was something else about Louise. Her busy daily schedule didn't hinder her from being an ardent soul winner. She often took ladies in the neighborhood to a Coffee

Hour Bible Study. But after a while it became evident that they were satisfied with their own religion. They had little interest in a personal relationship with the Lord.

Early one morning when Louise was praying in the living room, she remembered the story of the great supper in Luke 14. Those who were invited all made excuses, so the master sent his servant into the highways and hedges to compel others to come in.

Louise took it to the Lord in prayer. "Lord, the ones I have invited have made excuses; I would like to go to these others for You, but I'm here with my children. If You'll send someone to me from the highways and byways, I'll invite them to Your supper."

Right then she heard the beep-beep of a garbage truck backing up. Aha, that driver is from the highways and byways. She looked out the window and saw the man, now euphemistically called a sanitary engineer, lift the neighbor's trash container and empty it into the truck. It was obvious that his body was contorted as he did it. He was favoring himself, trying to ease some pain.

Louise stood by the curb when the truck pulled up at her house. As the driver, Reg, stepped out onto the pavement,

Louise asked him if he had a bad back. "No," he said. "A bad heart."

"Well, why are you handling heavy garbage cans all day?" she asked. "Here, I'll throw in mine," and she lifted the container and tipped its contents into the hopper of the truck.

The driver said, "It's the only job I can find."

"Well, I'll pray that you either get a better job or a better heart."

"Nobody cares about garbage men," said Reg sadly.

"God does," Louise replied.

Reg pulled himself into the cab of the truck and continued down the street.

A week later Louise was waiting at the curb when the truck arrived. Before Reg could get to the garbage can, Louise had emptied it into the truck. He looked at her and asked, "Did you pray for me?"

"Every day."

Reg didn't believe it although he didn't vocalize his doubt.

Louise continued, "Listen. The Bible says that faith without works is dead. I'm praying, but you have to apply for another job." He nodded, said nothing, and drove on.

On the next street, he saw Moira, Louise's second grader, who was on her way to school. As the truck stopped near her, she called out, "Hey, we pray for you at our house." Reg then knew that someone *did* care about garbage men.

A week later when Louise waited at the curb, Reg said, "Mrs. Nicholson. I believe in God and heaven and hell and all that, but there must be another step. Is there another step?"

Carefully Louise explained God's way of salvation to him and the importance of the step of faith. He listened intensely, then with a smile and a wave, he was off. She called after him, "Be sure and apply for that job."

For another week the Nicholsons prayed for Reg without fail. On garbage collection day, Louise was at her position by the curb. Reg was all smiles as he jumped down from the truck and said, "Well, I did it."

"Did what?" Did that mean that he had applied for a job?

"I took the step, Mrs. Nicholson." He explained that he had put his trust in the Lord Jesus.

Was it true? Had he really been saved? Louise thought, Well, whether it's true or not, he should read the Bible. After all, faith comes by hearing...the Word of God. "Reg, you need to start reading the Bible. It's like food for the soul."

"Aw, Mrs. Nicholson, you should have told me that sooner. If that's what a Christian has to do, I'm sorry. I'm no reader. I don't even read the newspaper. Sorry." And he drove down the street to the next house.

Around the next corner, he found a heavy box awaiting pickup. His curiosity compelled him to take a peek. There on the top was a brand new Bible, still in the clear plastic wrapper. "Alright, Lord, I'll read Your Book."

He not only began to read the Bible, he attended the church where the Nicholsons fellowship. He showed up in a flaming red jumpsuit, with the trash company's logo on the front. It was the best he had. There he was in the first row, grinning like a child in a candy store.

Everything suited him just right—the singing, the preaching, the friendliness of the people. When someone asked him why he attended the prayer meeting on Tuesday and another prayer meeting in a nearby assembly on Wednesday, he said, "I have to do double time. I have a lot of catching up to do."

Shortly after his conversion Reg was baptized. The Lord gave him victory over his alcohol habit. Not only did he attend the meetings faithfully, he brought his friends to hear the gospel. He enjoyed his salvation from day one.

His heart didn't improve, but he was able to find a less strenuous job for several years. Then the Lord called him home, a beloved brother in Christ, who had been called from the highways and byways and compelled to come to the great supper.

And all because a faithful housewife prayed, "Lord, use me."

Twenty-Nine

Time Would Fail to Tell it All

Every day throughout the world there are Christians who are showing what Jesus is like. "His image is not seen in the shape of their bodies, but in the beauty of the renewed mind and heart. Holiness, love, humility, kindness, and forgiveness—these make up the divine character."[26]

I have seen the Savior reproduced in lives of hospitality. How often have my host and hostess turned the master bedroom and bath over to me while they slept elsewhere. On one occasion, it was conference time, and a family had sixteen guests under their modest roof. The parents and three children slept in the garage. In Taiwan a missionary slept on the floor by the fireplace while I slept in his bed. He shed the glory by insisting that he had a warmer sleep than I did. He treated every guest as if he were Christ. A sister in Colorado was in a car wreck on the way to the morning service. Her injuries required immediate surgery. When she regained consciousness, her first words were, "Who's getting dinner for the visitors?"

When we think of the kindness of Jesus, our minds inevitably turn to His love of little children. To the disciples, they were a distraction and perhaps even a nuisance. Not to the Lord Jesus. To Him they were fit subjects for the kingdom of God. I have often suspected that He was more comfortable with little children than with adults.

Sadhu Sundar Singh modeled his Lord. Often when he was a guest in a home, he got down on the floor and played with the children. One night some children asked, "Mother, may Jesus put us to bed tonight." They had seen Jesus in Singh.

Another incident tells a similar story. A man in a hurry carelessly bumped into a young lad whose arms were filled with bundles, then scolded him as if it was the boy's fault. Another passerby saw what had happened, helped pick up the bundles, and gave the boy a dollar bill, saying, "I hope this will repay you for what has happened."

The youngster, a stranger to that sort of kindness, asked, "Sir, are you Jesus?" "No," the Christian replied, "but I'm one of His followers."

Other believers display Christlikeness by their restraint under provocation. A missionary in Quito was involved in an accident. A woman turning left from the right lane smashed into the side of his car. When they got out of their cars, she screamed at him, insulted his race and nation, then slapped him on the face. As he returned to his car, he thanked the Lord for the fruit of the Spirit called self-control. He said, "While there was only minimal damage to my car, I have to confess that for the next few days, I found myself wondering how I might have responded if I did not have the Lord."

Dr. Ida Scudder, a missionary doctor in India for many years, had a non-retaliatory spirit. A Muslim once asked her why this was so. Before she could answer, a Hindu friend, who knew Dr. Scudder, provided the answer. "Don't you know why? It's because Dr. Ira's God is patient and loving, and she's like her God."[27]

We love the Lord Jesus for His kindness and compassion to those of low estate, and we love to see it in His people. Borden of Yale, reared in a home of wealth and luxury, was sometimes found washing dishes in a skid row mission. When a British evangelist was returning home, someone asked him, "What impressed you most in the United States?" He answered, "Seeing William Borden, that son of millionaires, with his arm around a bum at the city mission."

Paul Sandberg was another one who had not followed his Master in vain. One day he entered a coffee shop, sat on a stool, and struck up a conversation with the fellow next to him. Paul, a noted singer, faithfully witnessed to Fred and eventually had the privilege of leading him to the Lord. After some weeks, Fred was stricken with terminal cancer. Paul visited him regularly in a sub-standard nursing home, performing the duties that the nurse's aides should have done. The night Fred died, Paul was holding him in his arms, and quoting verses of Scripture. I call that compassion.

When a small Christian fellowship in Japan decided to build a chapel, they went around to all the neighbors with the plans to see if anyone objected. No one did. But before the work was actually started they heard that there was a man who was afraid the chapel would block the sunlight coming into his yard. The Christians didn't find fault with him for not objecting sooner. Instead they paid the architect to redesign the building with a lower roof. The neighbor was pleased and puzzled: pleased that he would get his sunlight, and puzzled by the gracious spirit of the Christians.

If we are like the Lord Jesus, we will have love and consideration for people of all positions in life. It was customary in the Elliot family to have devotions at the breakfast table. One morning when the father was reading the Bible to the others, he heard the garbage cans rattling in the yard. Immediately he put the Bible aside, opened the window, and called out a cheery greeting to the garbage collector. To him neither activity was more sacred than the other was. He made no distinction between the sacred and the secular.

Christ is modeled in every walk of life. A businessman said of a Christian competitor, "You don't need a written contract when you deal with him. His word is enough." That contractor never wrote out a contract with his customers.

A soccer referee said, "When I am refereeing a game in which Tommy Walker is playing, I have only twenty-one players to watch, not twenty-two." Tommy would never break the rules.

When a tax consultant told a client not to declare a large amount of income, assuring him that the government would never know, the Christian said, "I must declare it. I'm a Christian." His faith affected his finances.

Shortly after he was saved, a used car salesman told a prospective customer, "I don't have anything on the lot that I would sell to you." That is not typical salesmanship on a used car lot.

A Christian doctor refused to sign a false insurance claim for a patient, and brought down a torrent of verbal abuse on himself. A missionary's luggage was held up in customs because the agent wanted a bribe and the missionary wouldn't pay it.

After a believer has made a verbal agreement to sell his home for $250,000, another prospective buyer comes along and offers $265,000. What should he do? The answer is in Psalm 15:4. The person who dwells with God *"swears to his own hurt and does not change."* Better to lose $15,000 than to lose your integrity. Better to have the same religion on Monday that you have on Sunday.

Sometimes we see Christlikeness in those who triumph over trial. A Christian couple finally had a baby after years of waiting. Sadly, however, the baby died of apnea (crib death) a few months later. The minister said, "What really challenged me and stirred me was the singing of a hymn at the church. *Ascribe Greatness to Our God, the Rock.* I saw the woman standing with her husband, the tears streaming down her face, but with her face aglow and lifted up to God. And she was singing:

> Ascribe greatness to our God, the Rock,
> His work is perfect and all His ways are just.
> A God of faithfulness, and without injustice,
> Good and upright is He.

I am reminded also of the case of Beverly West. The doctor had just told her that she had terminal cancer. And right at that time, she heard that Gary Wilson was in the hospital with a serious case of pancreatitis. So she sat down and wrote the following:

Our dear Gary, Beth, and family. We want you to know that you are in our prayers daily and throughout the day. May you know the comfort of the everlasting arms around you. You are held by His strength and grace.

Since I was recently diagnosed with terminal cancer and now am on chemo, I have much time to pray. You are at the top of the list.

Someone, Amy Carmichael in *Gold by Moonlight*, I believe, pointed out that in Philippians 3:10 the power of His resurrection comes before the fellowship of His suffering. May we all come to know Christ in these ways. It is a privilege to understand a little of the fellowship of Gethsemane and the Cross and to be enabled to say by His power, *'Not my will, but Thine be done.'*

> In His bonds of love,
> John and Beverly"

On a lighter note. When a doctor told a Christian that one of his eyes had to be removed and a glass eye installed in its place, he said, "Please, doctor, put one in with a twinkle in it." That, friends, is victory through submission.

Someone has written, "How exhilarating it is to think that we can model the qualities of Christ to those who are searching for Him. By an exemplary lifestyle, the disciple can make his or her Lord attractive to others. In his letter to Titus, Paul urged him to teach slaves to please their masters *'so that in every way they will make the teaching about God our Savior attractive'* (Titus 2:10, NIV). People should not only hear truth worth hearing but see truth worth emulating."

Thirty
Living Above the Average

Michelangelo stood silently in his studio, gazing intently at a block of marble. Finally a companion interrupted his reverie by asking why he was spending so much time gazing at the rough block. Michelangelo's face lit up as he said with enthusiasm, "There's an angel in that block and I'm going to liberate him."

There is a spiritual parallel here. Christ indwells every child of God. The apostle Paul said to the Colossians, *"Christ in you, the hope of glory"* (Colossians 1:27). In Galatians 2:20 he made it clear that Christ lives in believers. But the world cannot see Him unless He is liberated. This happens when we Christians display Him by a life of godliness. It happens when we speak and act as the Lord would. It happens when the Lord Jesus Christ is allowed to live out His life through us.

Displaying Christ to the world should not be confined to isolated acts of godly behavior. It should be our way of life, our characteristic mode. The trouble with many of us is that our spiritual reflexes are too slow. A wonderful opportunity comes for us to respond by a life that is above the ordinary. It isn't until later that we think of how brilliantly we could have spoken or acted as Jesus would have done. But we missed it. We didn't rise above flesh and blood.

Most people have never rejected the Lord Jesus. They have rejected our representation of Him: our short temper, our sarcastic words, our covetousness, and our pride. They don't see His love, His courtesy, and His graciousness in us.

How can we consistently model Christ to a world that neither sees or knows Him? How can we live above the average? We can cultivate the mind of Christ by humility, servanthood, unselfishness, and esteeming others better than ourselves. We can dwell *"in the secret place of the Most High"* (Psalm 91:1) by staying close to the Lord, by living in the sanctuary rather than in the suburbs. We can be constantly occupied with the Lord.

"We all, with unveiled face, beholding as in a mirror the

glory of the Lord, are being transformed into the same image from glory to glory, just as by the Spirit of the Lord" (2 Corinthians 3:18).

The more we gaze on the Lord in the Bible, the more the Holy Spirit transforms us into His likeness.

Endnotes

1 Major Ian Thomas, quoted in *His Victorious Indwelling*, Nick Harrison, ed., Grand Rapids, MI: Zondervan Publishing House, 1999, pp. 133-134.

2 *The Idiot*, Ware, Herts, England, 1996.

3 Adapted from the following two books:

—*Brother Indeed*, Frank Holmes, London: Victory Press, 1959.

—*Chief Men Among the Brethren*, Hy Pickering, London: Pickering & Inglis, 1931.

4 Quoted from *In All Their Afflictions*, Murdoch Campbell, Resolis, Scotland: Self-published, n.d., pp. 90-91.

5 Adapted from *The Way of Peace*, H. A. Ironside, New York: Loizeaux Brothers, 1940, pp. 176-177.

6 Adapted from tape #150 *Flirting with the Truth*, Ravi Zacharias.

7 Adapted from *Our Daily Bread*, Grand Rapids, MI: Radio Bible Class, reading for June 28, 1995. Also from tape by Lloyd Oppel, Feb. 5, 2000.

8 Adapted from *The Flying Scotsman*, Sally Magnusson, New York: Quartet Books, 1981, and miscellaneous clippings.

9 *The Flying Scotsman,* pp. 9-10.

10 *The Flying Scotsman,* pp. 163-164.

11 *The Flying Scotsman,* p. 174.

12 Adapted from *Philippians, The Gospel at Work,* Merrill C. Tenney, Grand Rapids, MI: Wm. B. Eerdman Publishing Co., 1956, p. 60.

13 Adapted from "Living by Vows," *Christianity Today,* October 8, 1990, pp. 38-90 and "Muriel's Blessing," *Christianity Today,* February 5, 1996. Both articles by Robertson McQuilken.

14 Adapted from letter by Jim Haesemeyer.

15 *Tragedy to Triumph,* Frank Retief, Milton Keynes, England: Word Publishing, 1994, p. 148.

16 *The Pilgrim,* E. Schuyler English, ed., Vol. IX, No. 4, April 1952, p. 2.

17 London: Banner of Truth Trust, 1970, p. 149.

18 Adapted from tape #118 *Raised to Run* by Ravi Zacharias

19 *Tramp for the Lord,* Corrie Ten Boom, Old Tappan, NJ: Fleming H. Revell Co., 1974, pp. 53-54.

20 One or two of the illustrations in this book are composites, combining the experience of more than one person.

21 Adapted from *Gladys Aylward. The Little Woman,* Gladys Aylward as told to Christine Hunter, Chicago, IL.: Moody Press, pp. 109-120.

22 Adapted from tape #118 *Raised to Run: Jacob* by Ravi Zacharias.

23 Adapted from *John Nelson Darby,* Max S. Weremchuk, Neptune, NJ.: Loizeaux Bros, 1992, pp. 149-150.

24 Adapted from *Our Daily Bread,* August 23, 2000.

25 Used with permission of Louise and J. B. Nicholson, Jr.

26 Daily Notes of the Scripture Union. Further documentation unavailable.

27 Adapted from *Our Daily Bread,* February 9, 1993.

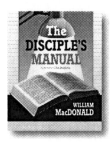
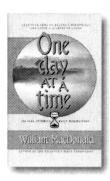

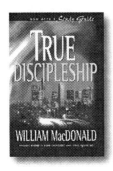

TRUE DISCIPLESHIP w/ STUDY GUIDE

This book clearly explains the principles of New Testament discipleship. The Saviour's terms of discipleship are not only highly practical and will reward in knowing the peace that passes understanding.

Binding: Paper   Page Count: 208
Category: Christian Living   ISBN: 1882701917

OUR GOD IS WONDERFUL

A devotional which proclaims the wonder of God. The three sections this book covers are: His amazing creation from the vastness of the universe to the marvel of the living cell, His provisions for believers in times of need, and the ends to which He will go to redeem lost sinners.

Binding: Paper   Page Count: 160
Category: Devotional   ISBN: 1882701607

THE WONDERS OF GOD

In this devotional, the author presents an array of evidence—from creation, providence, and redemption—that God is the most wonderful Person in the universe. Know Him better, love Him more through this stirring real-life drama all around us.

Binding: Paper   Page Count: 120
Category: Devotional   ISBN: 1882701259

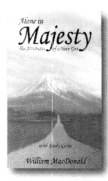

ALONE IN MAJESTY w/ STUDY GUIDE

Explores God's characteristics—those unique to Him and those shared with humanity. With this in-depth Bible study you will gain greater knowledge of God's attributes.

Binding: paper
Category: Devotional

Page Count: 310
ISBN: 1893579077

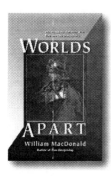

WORLDS APART

A doctrinal book that compares the principles of the kingdom of the world and the kingdom of God. The believer is faced each day with choices which reveal his loyalty to each of these two kingdoms.

Binding: Paper
Category: Doctrinal

Page Count: 80
ISBN: 1882701054

NOW THAT IS AMAZING GRACE

The well-loved classic, Amazing Grace, has stirred the hearts of millions. William MacDonald takes the reader on a thrilling expedition to discover the breathtaking heights and depths of God's amazing grace.

Binding: Paper
Category: Christian
Living/Doctrinal

Page Count: 96
ISBN: 1882701216

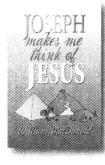

JOSEPH MAKES ME THINK OF JESUS

A biography of the life of Joseph and commentary which outlines the correspondences between his life and that of the Lord Jesus.

Binding: Paper
Category: Commentary/ Bible Biography

Page Count: 144
ISBN: 1882701690

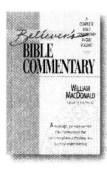

BELIEVER'S BIBLE COMMENTARY

A complete Bible commentary in one volume! A thorough, yet easy to read Bible commentary that turns complicated theology into practical understanding.

Binding: Cloth
Category: Commentary

Page Count: 2464
ISBN: 0840719728

Enjoy your Bible	ISBN: 1882701585
Here's the Difference	ISBN: 1882701453
Once in Christ, in Christ Forever	ISBN: 1882701437
The Forgotten Command: Be Holy	ISBN: 0946351376
My Heart, My Life, My All	ISBN: 1882701445

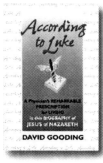

CPSIA information can be obtained
at www.ICGtesting.com
Printed in the USA
FFOW03n1216140318
45568518-46349FF